RADICAL ROOTS

A Collection of Paintings, Stories, and Poems
Celebrating the 500th Anniversary of Anabaptist Origins

GARETH BRANDT

Foreword by John E. Sharp

RADICAL ROOTS
A Collection of Paintings, Stories, and Poems
Celebrating the 500ᵗʰ Anniversary of Anabaptist Origins

by Gareth Brandt
Foreword by John E. Sharp

Copyright © 2024
All rights reserved.

All rights reserved. Reproduction or utilization of this work in any form, by any means now known or herein after invented, including but not limited to xerography, photocopying and recording, and in any storage and retrieval system, is forbidden without permission from the copyrighted holder.

Library of Congress Control Number: 2024939120
International Standard Book Number: 978-1-60126-934-8

219 Mill Road | Morgantown, PA 19543-9516
www.Masthof.com

DEDICATION

This book is dedicated to all the students in my Anabaptist History and Thought class over the years. Please insert your name here if you were one of those students and are reading this. Most of you entered the course without much intrinsic motivation and some of you left the course having been transformed with new perspectives and commitments to new ways of being. Your engagement and interaction have left me transformed and forever grateful.

LAND ACKNOWLEDGEMENT

It is important to note that at the very same time the Anabaptist movement was having its beginnings in continental Europe in the 16th century, other Europeans were in a race to explore and colonize distant continents, one of which my European ancestors came to hundreds of years later. Mennonites were sometimes persecuted and landless people in Europe and were grateful for safety and opportunity on a new continent, often unaware that they were being given land taken forcefully and deceptively from Indigenous people who had lived there and thrived off the land since time immemorial. Because European Mennonite settlers have benefitted from colonialism, I see the work of decolonization, reparation, and reconciliation with our Indigenous hosts as important work for Anabaptists at 500.[1] I am grateful to be living in the ancestral, traditional, and unceded territory of the Stó:lō people on the Pacific Northwest coast of our continent.

TABLE OF CONTENTS

Foreword by John E. Sharp vii
Introduction..1

Christendom 5
The Diet of Worms 9
The School of Heretics 13
A Baptism of Choice 17
The Gate of Nuremberg 21
Third Baptism 25
Chains...29
The Road to Schleitheim 33
Castle Church 37
Jacob Hutter's Prison 41
Easter Worship Service 45
Menno's First Church..51
The Cages of Münster 55
Menno's Motto 61
Strasbourg 67

Anabaptist Origins Timeline 70
Bibliography...78
Endnotes...79
Acknowledgements 81
About the Author 83

FOREWORD

Gareth Brandt presents here a feast for heart, mind, and soul. Far more than an esoteric litany of historical facts, this book is the story of a spiritual heritage, which the author has embraced, reconsidered, reinterpreted—and continues to question.

Having been a teacher of Anabaptist history and thought for nearly two decades in the classroom, the pulpit, and on the road as a tour leader, Brandt crafts a narrative seasoned beautifully with paintings and poetry.

The author, recognizing the danger of a single narrative, probes multiple sources and origin stories to create a story far more complex than the one-dimensional story I learned from the Benderian school of thought at Goshen. The next generation of scholars explored the religious and spiritual dimensions in their social, economic, political, and historical contexts. Ever thoughtful and contemplative, Brandt continues the multidimensional narrative that is both celebratory and instructive.

It is a complex story, but more than that, Brandt is committed to living the vision in its more radical expressions. In defining "radical" he wrests it away from the violence by which it is often characterized today and takes us back to the roots—to Jesus and the Anabaptists' response to Jesus.

Radical and practical. Brandt is both. Ever the teacher and preacher he asks his readers to ponder the meaning of this story. Why and in what way is it significant for us today? How does it shape our attempts to live, teach, and witness for peace?

Gareth has asked me to reflect on my son's witness for peace. Michael "MJ" Sharp spent the last eight years of his young life as a reconciling presence on army bases in Germany and in the forests of the Democratic Republic of the Congo

(DRC). For the Military Counseling Network, a Mennonite Mission Network assignment, he walked with U.S. soldiers who were transformed by the senseless killing on the battlefield and became conscientious objectors. With Mennonite Central Committee in the DRC, MJ forged relationships with displaced people in camps and negotiated with warlords in the forests. As an Armed Group Expert for the UN, he investigated sanctions violations and tracked illegal arms trading.

For shorter periods, MJ also worked in the West Bank, Iraq, and Afghanistan.

While working in the DRC, he told us he had no death wish. On the other hand, he said he was not afraid to die. This may have given him the courage to approach and question the armed and masked men in the act of robbing passengers of a high-jacked bus. After hearing a series of MJ's questions, they just walked away. Many other stories can be told.

On March 12, 2017, he and Swedish colleague Zaida Catalan embarked on their final mission. On the trail to visit a new militia, MJ and Zaida were abducted and shot to death. He was 34; she was 36. She was investigating the well-being of child soldiers, and it seems MJ was about to expose a gun-running operation of a national army colonel who is now in prison.

Since then, some have speculated that these two may be heroes or martyrs. Indeed, they gave their lives working for the shalom of the Congolese people. I won't speculate. For Michele and me, he is simply our son; for Erin and Laura, he is simply their brother, much loved and missed daily.

Their story and this book, call us to work and pray for peace and reconciliation wherever we live, work, and play.

- John E. Sharp
Hesston, KS
On the feast day of St. Justin Martyr
1 June 2024

INTRODUCTION

Who were and are the Anabaptists? What happened 500 years ago that was so significant? Why does the Anabaptist movement still matter today? Why is it worthy of a celebration? I hope that by the time you get to the end of this book, these questions will have been addressed. The origins of the Anabaptist movement in Europe 500 years ago are important for people like me who cherish a spiritual heritage that has its roots in this movement. While I believe that all spiritual traditions have contributions to make to each other and to the wider world, because we live in a time of escalating state-sanctioned violence, I believe a tradition like Anabaptism that has always questioned and critiqued church relationships with the state, has a unique and increasingly relevant voice. Stuart Murray asks, "Could it be, as some have suggested, that Anabaptism is a vision whose time has come?"[2] He, along with other historians are beginning to "take Anabaptism more seriously as a radical renewal movement that might have considerable contemporary significance."[3] Our times are very different from what they were like 500 years ago in Europe, but perhaps the stories of Anabaptist origins can continue to inspire and be a witness in our time.

The exact origins of the Anabaptist movement are as hard to hit as a moving target. It was a movement after all! As will be noted by the stories following, there have been attempts made; yet there is no unanimous agreement among scholars as to the precise nature and development of the Anabaptist movement.[4] Although the baptismal service of January 21, 1525, in Zurich, Switzerland, is often seen as the inaugural event of Anabaptism and the one that has set off all kinds of 500th anniversary events and publications, the stories in this book range from 1522 to 1536 and happened in different geographical regions of central Europe: Switzerland, southern Germany, the Tyrol region of Austria, the former province of Moravia in present-day Czechia, the Netherlands, and northern Germany. History is not an exact science; it is an interpretation of events; literally, the telling of a story. The story of Anabaptist origins is one worth telling even if it can be best described as a polygenesis[5] (many beginnings) with multiple leaders, locations, events, and ideals. Those varied and messy origins might even be part of its appeal and ongoing significance!

As a later story will indicate, the Anabaptist movement can be seen as rooted in medieval Catholic mysticism just as much as in modern Protestant biblicism, yet it has sometimes been described as the radical wing of the Reformation. I like the word "radical" to describe the Anabaptist movement even if the usage of the word has sometimes taken on some dangerous implications of late. I choose to redeem the word for the purposes of this book. A dictionary definition is not always helpful for historical or theological purposes, but in this case it is.

"1: of, relating to, or proceeding from a root. 2a: a root part; b: a basic principle. 3a: marked by a considerable departure from the usual or traditional; b: tending or disposed to make extreme changes in existing views, habits, conditions, or institutions."[6]

It is "3b" that has come into recent usage when describing dangerous extremes of political or religious ideologies. News commentators speak of those who have been "radicalized" as having dedicated themselves so zealously to a cause that they are willing to brazenly kill and be killed for it.

I grew up in the 1960s and 70s when "3a" was the common understanding of the word; for my generation it was a badge of honor to be called unusual and non-traditional. Perhaps this influenced me towards using it in my title. This definition is still used in informal conversation to describe people who dress or act differently than the majority. "That outfit is radical" means that it is provocative and unusual.

Most people are probably unaware of the first definitions, which derive most directly from the Latin *"radix"* meaning literally, root. Thus, the title of the book is in that sense redundant, although my intent is to combine all definitions!

The 16th-century Anabaptist movement was an attempt to recover the "roots" of early Christianity. The Anabaptists looked primarily to the example of Jesus in the Gospels and to descriptions of the early church such as the one in Acts 2:42-47 where the church is marked by obedience to the teaching of Jesus and mutual sharing. How well they did in this attempt is open to evaluation. In doing this, Anabaptism broke from the usual and traditional way of being church at the time that was marked by outward displays of pomp and power. In the enthusiasm for changing the corrupted traditional forms of church, Anabaptists in the 16th century sometimes became extreme, bizarre, and even violent. The stories in this book will illustrate all three definitions of radical. The Anabaptists were not the first or the last to be labeled radical. Numerous other Christian movements in medieval and modern times have also attempted to be radical in a similar way.[7]

I have appreciated J. Denny Weaver's retelling of the Anabaptist origins story in his text, *Becoming Anabaptist,* over the past 17 years of teaching Anabaptist History and Thought to undergraduate students. It not only tells the story of how people first became Anabaptist in the 16th century but also challenges readers to think about why the movement is still significant today. Every year I taught the course, I read from the foreword to introduce the course. The foreword was written by William H. Willimon, who according to his title at the time, seems quite traditional: "Bishop, The North Alabama Conference of the United Methodist Church." He captures well the essence of the Anabaptist movement.

"This book is a clinch-fisted protest against what the rest of us have made of the church, a defiant act of resistance against the predominant [North] American way of being Christian, a song of love (disconcerting thought—Mennonites making love) to a Jesus that the rest of us are reluctant to follow and a people who, in every generation, Jesus has loved into being out of nothing. To subvert the present ecclesiastical order, Weaver on nearly every page of this book lures us into a respectful discussion of how Anabaptists got here

and what they believe. Typical of the Mennonites I have known, he politely reassures us that he is a pacifist Christian who bears us no harm, then hands us a ticking bomb."[8]

What you hold in your hands is not a ticking bomb of prophetic challenge or an eloquent scholarly tome; it is a simple picture book of stories and poems that celebrates the 500th anniversary of a radical movement. Yet I hope it will be more than quaint folk art and whimsical poetry to adorn Mennonite coffee tables—I hope it provides some inspiration and provocation toward radical faith and love in our own time. At the least, some gratitude for a spiritual heritage that has changed lives and communities over the last 500 years.

This book is not meant to be an exhaustive introduction to Anabaptist history or even a summary of main events in Anabaptist origins. It simply follows my literal journeys on a few Anabaptist Heritage Tours in Europe. These visits to historical sites where things happened have been about much more than satisfying my historical curiosity or increasing my knowledge—they have been transformative experiences.[9] They have been a spiritual pilgrimage. I hope to offer a small taste of these experiences in this book as my contribution to the celebration of a radical religious heritage. I hope that this book can be part of a reader's own spiritual pilgrimage, not unlike how John Ruth saw himself a pilgrim upon visiting the sites where significant things happened 500 years ago:

"Envision, now, a traveler from a North American Mennonite family meditating among the monuments of [Europe, five centuries after Anabaptists] risked their earthly citizenship for a heavenly one… Here, he reflects, is where so much that he lives by was first proclaimed, later to be clarified and refined in the fires of persecution. Baptism deliberately and joyfully accepted as the beginning of a new life, the Lord's Supper as an expression of [community], abandonment of hopelessly rooted human violence, the freeing of the church from all loyalties but the Rule of Christ…"[10]

As the reader contemplates the places and people of the Anabaptist movement in picture, prose, and poetry, it is hoped that they might gratefully recognize themselves as part of a larger movement and be inspired to continue on their journey of following Jesus.

Since the central act of the Anabaptist movement was believer's water baptism, it seemed appropriate to paint scenes with water. The paintings are in a simple folk-art style that is symbolic of the Anabaptist/Mennonite value of simplicity and non-adornment. In the same spirit, the frames, backing, and mattes were all purchased from an MCC Thrift Store and/or made by hand from leftover or found materials. There will be fifteen paintings, each followed by a story of what happened there in the 16th century and what I experienced in the 21st century, then a poem and/or selected quotes (sometimes my paraphrases) that pertain to the people or events related to the painting.

"CHRISTENDOM"

When Mennonite pilgrims from the rest of the world travel to Europe to visit sites related to the Anabaptist movement, they only find a few simple plaques, small cairns, and tombstones. Therefore, these pilgrimage tours must fill their itineraries with visits to the impressive castles and ornate cathedrals of Christendom. Ironically, it was the Christendom marriage of church and state, and subsequent tithes and taxes that provided funds to build these cathedrals; furthermore, it was the Christendom establishment that was responsible for persecuting the Anabaptists!

I have sometimes heard people say how these grand cathedrals inspire worship or that the ornate statues and windows with biblical scenes were created so that the illiterate masses could still participate in the stories of the Gospel. But I wonder how I would respond if I was a poor peasant coming on my annual pilgrimage to the cathedral, knowing that my tax and tithe money had built this impressive structure while my family at home was starving. Perhaps I would have joined the Peasants' Revolt instead or felt more at home in an Anabaptist worship service in a cave or barn.

I could have painted any number of cathedrals to symbolize the era of Christendom from the fifth to the sixteenth century that was dominated by the union of church and state. This one in Bacharach, Germany, is not one of the largest or most spectacular but was simply chosen for the view downward from a hilltop and toward the Rhine valley. The prominent steeple and the tall orientation are characteristic of the glory of Christendom, but rather "unanabaptist!"

The Formation of Christendom

I suppose we could say Jesus started it all because He did mention a kingdom.

"Now is the time! Here comes God's kingdom! Change your hearts and lives and trust this good news!" (Jesus in Mark 1:15)

"All of us [who follow Jesus] throughout the whole world have traded in our weapons of war. We have exchanged our swords for plowshares, our spears for farm tools… Now we cultivate the fear of God, justice, kindness, faith, and the expectation of the future given us through the crucified one… The more we are persecuted and martyred, the more do others in ever increasing numbers become believers." (Justin Martyr, 165)

But something began to happen in the 4th century as emperors presided over church councils, pagan holy days were Christianized, and baptism became a rite of citizenship.

"We are pleased to allow Christians the right to exist and to set up places of worship; provided always that they do not offend against the public order. It will be the duty of Christians to pray to their God for our recovery, for the public wealth and for their own; that the state may be preserved from danger on every side, and that they themselves may dwell safely in their homes." (The Edict of Toleration or Edict of Milan, 311).

"It is our desire that all the various nations which are subject to our clemency and moderation, should continue in the profession of that religion which was delivered to the Romans by the divine Apostle Peter… We authorize the followers of this law to assume the title of Catholic Christians… but the others… shall be branded with the ignominious name of heretics." (Edict by Emperor Theodosius making Christianity the official religion of the empire, 380)

Christians who had once been persecuted became the persecutors and took up the sword to defend and spread the Christian faith.

"If there is anyone of the Saxon people lurking among them unbaptized, and if he scorns to come to baptism and stay a pagan, let him die." (Charlemagne's instructions to his soldiers in their conquests of northern Europe, 800)

"Enter upon the road to the Holy Sepulchre; wrest that land from the wicked race, and subject it to yourselves … God has conferred upon you above all nations great glory in arms. Accordingly undertake this journey for the remission of your sins, with the assurance of the imperishable glory of the Kingdom of Heaven … Let this then be your war-cry in combats because this word is given to you by God. When an armed attack is made upon the enemy, let this one cry be raised by all the soldiers of God: It is the will of God! It is the will of God!" (Pope Urban II in his speech to encourage the soldiers of the First Crusade, 1095)

"Nicholas, The Roman pontiff, successor of the key-bearer of the heavenly kingdom and vicar of Jesus Christ, contemplating with a father's mind all the several climes of the world and seeking and desiring the salvation of all… This we believe will more certainly come to pass, through the aid of the Lord, if we bestow suitable favors and special graces on those kings and princes… to invade, search out, capture, vanquish, and subdue all Saracens and pagans whatsoever, and other enemies of Christ wheresoever placed… and to capture and claim all movable and immovable goods whatsoever held and possessed by them and to reduce their persons to perpetual slavery, and to apply and appropriate to himself and his successors the kingdoms, dominions, possessions, and goods, and to convert them to his and their use and profit." (Bulls of Discovery issued by Pope Nicholas V, 1454)

Over the years they got the nature of Jesus' kingdom wrong. The Anabaptists seemed to recognize this 500 years ago. What about us today?

"Love your enemies. Do good to those who hate you. Treat people in the same way that you want them to treat you." (Jesus in Luke 6:27,31)[11]

"THE DIET OF WORMS"

The Anabaptist movement may not have happened if it had not been for the courageous stand of Martin Luther. Luther appeared before the diet ("assembly") gathered in the city of Worms in 1521 to defend the charges of heresy brought on by his initial confrontation of church abuses at Wittenberg. His words in response to the charges have become famous: "Here I stand, I can do no other."

This is the Lutheran Church in Worms; it is just as impressive as many Roman Catholic cathedrals. Anabaptists like to be known as a third way, neither Catholic nor Protestant. Roman Catholics and Protestant Reformers were both aligned with various states, they both practiced infant baptism that signified citizenship as well as faith, and they both wielded the sword for the protection of land and church. Anabaptists felt that the church should not be involved in any of the above; thus, a third way.

At the same time, I would say that Anabaptist roots are both Catholic and Protestant. Catholic in the sense that Anabaptism had much in common with medieval mysticism and monasticism; they just felt that all Christians should practice the rigorous discipleship in all of life what was practiced in the seclusion of monasteries by a few. And it is fair to argue that Catholic scholar Erasmus had more influence on Anabaptist theology than Luther. Yet the Anabaptists were Protestant in the sense that they were indeed protesting the corruptions of Christendom with a spirit of reform based on an appeal to Scripture and a response of faith that Luther and others championed before them.

Martin Luther

Martin Luther
opened up a can of worms
in Wittenberg on Halloween
of fifteen seventeen
and let them crawl all o'r the door—
all ninety-five of them!

Martin Luther
learned you dare not disagree
with powers that be
on their official doctrine
and not expect a din;
so they invited him to dinner
at the diet of worms
where they said

"Martin Luther,
you can't say this sort of thing and stay
in the holy sanctum," and he said,
"Well, I said it and I'm not sorry
and here I stand,
so let that be scribed"—
and it was.

Martin Luther,
we are thankful
that you opened up the can
despite the cacophony caused
your stand has stood
the times of sand.

Menno on Luther

I know there are a great many who will ask why I, an unlearned man, am not satisfied in regard to this matter with the doctrine of Martin Luther and other renowned doctors... I acknowledge and also solemnly confess before you and the whole world that they and many others are well gifted with learning, eloquence, subtlety, languages, and science, and that I, poor, ignorant man, in comparison with them, am less than a fly is to an elephant. Therefore, I am heartily ashamed to write and speak against them with my dull pen and awkward speech. Yet every reader should know that however learned the beforementioned scholars are, and however ignorant I am, yet our opinions are all worth about equally much before God, for without the command of the holy Scripture nothing righteous can be done and nothing pleasing to God can be practiced, let him be whosoever he may. The holy Scriptures do not refer us to them nor to any other learned person, but to Jesus Christ alone.

(Menno Simons, "Christian Baptism"[12])

"THE SCHOOL OF HERETICS"

I grew up thinking Mennonites were a bunch of old, out-of-touch traditionalists, but in college, when I first heard the story about the students of Ulrich Zwingli in Zurich, I gained a whole new perspective. The Anabaptist movement was in many respects a radical youth movement as most of these students were in their early twenties! It all began when Andreas Castelberger started a Bible study group that included Felix Manz, George Blaurock, and Conrad Grebel. I was particularly drawn to Conrad Grebel, a university student trying to find himself and his faith as he drifted from one university to another. They came to be aptly nicknamed "The School of Heretics" as they took Zwingli's teaching further than he ever intended. (The same thing has sometimes happened with my students and young adult children!)

When walking around in the Grossmunster ("large church") in Zurich, Switzerland, I came to this darkened alcove with a semi-circle of seats and a lectern and imagined that this was where the "school" met to learn, debate, and discuss. The back lighting and the space away from the main sanctuary seemed to fit the clandestine and radical nature of the early meetings of this radical circle of young university students. Photos were not permitted but in the spirit of subversion I was able to discreetly snap a few photos to guide me in this painting.

Sonnet for the School of Heretics

What did you learn about in that fine school?
Why in a circle instead of straight rows?
Will not your questions make you be a fool?
Do you think rebellion makes your faith grow?

These are the questions we put to you now:
Andreas, Conrad, and Felix, and George
Who to no empire would cater and bow
Did you know then a new church you would forge?

University dropouts with wonder lust
We revere you now; name schools after you
And we consider you founders of us
But what would you say now? What shall we do?

Don't be afraid; confront powers that be
God's justice and peace will finally reign free.

Youthful Enthusiasm or Prophetic Challenge?

I just can't shut up! God's Word will decide the truth about baptism, the Lord's Supper, and the Sword. You know the Bible by all sorts of research and exegesis much better than I do, but I pray that you would also learn to simply obey it. Too many old traditions stagnate the freshness of the Spirit.

The letter you sent with the booklet is like a slap in the face! God will judge me if I have been a rebel and a troublemaker. I know that you leaders and pastors deserve respect, but let God judge us by our fruits.

Do not get the wrong idea that I am angry; please accept this in a spirit of friendship.

(Author's paraphrase of Conrad Grebel's letter to Vadian, his mentor and brother-in-law, December 15, 1524.[13])

"A BAPTISM OF CHOICE"

There had already been a series of disputations about believer's baptism vs. infant baptism when a group of Zurich radicals met in the upper room of Felix Manz's mother's house on the evening of January 21, 1525. The fact that Conrad Grebel had a young daughter who was still not baptized—and subsequently not a tax-paying citizen—probably added to the tense mood of the meeting. As they met that evening, they were quite aware of the possible severe consequences of their stand on baptism. Nervousness must have given way to excitement as George Blaurock blurted out that Conrad should baptize him here and now as a sign of adult commitment to Christ and to each other. Blaurock in turn baptizes others who are present. As the baptismal service continues, they surely have no idea that in this bold act they inaugurated a community of faith that would eventually spread beyond Europe to every other continent.

We know that this event happened on "Neustadt-Gasse," a short alley in the shadows of the Grossmünster. On this short street is this fountain in the foreground of the picture, which dates back to before the 16th century and is the likely water source for that first believer's baptism ceremony, which may have been held in the upper room of the house in the background. Although Anabaptists generally do not believe in relics or "holy water," it is interesting how many seasoned Mennonites I have seen sticking their heads under the fountain, washing themselves or even collecting a small vial of water to take home! Indeed, it was exciting for me to read an account of this baptismal service on site.[14]

500th Anniversary
Part 1

The evening of January
twenty-first, fifteen, twenty-five
a group of radicals took a dive;
not into a tank or lake or river—
that would have been a shiver
in Zurich during winter.

That evening of January,
instead, was done quite secretly,
for it was a forbidden act
and a sober communal pact
to separate from powers that be
to form a church that would be free
from Christendom
with which they just could not jive.

Re-Baptism Rant

Unfortunately sometimes nicknames stick whether you like them or not in this case the nickname was re-baptizers but it was meant as a slam it was meant to damn because baptism meant citizenship taxes and most importantly salvation and of course political control which went unstated so basically what the nickname meant to say was that you're out of control you're unwilling to conform you're an illegal alien you're a traitor and you're going straight to hell whereas the so nicknamed all they wanted to be called is brothers and sisters in Christ in other words that they were kin and needed no king no king but Christ for them it was not about conquering territory for Christ or going into all the world for Christ or for getting all your doctrines right about Christ but it was about choosing to follow Jesus in your life for Christ's sake it's as simple as that in the every-day and in the nitty-gritty and the itty-bitty so let's not get all out of joint about sprinkled or poured or dribbled or dipped or dunked or drowned or once or twice or even thrice or young or old or teen or in-between it is getting extreme because by now it all seems to be a grand adventure in missing the point!

"THE GATE OF NUREMBERG"

Unbeknownst to those gathered in Zurich, something else happened on that very same day—January 21, 1525—some miles and a mountain range away in Nuremberg, Germany. Hans Denck, rector of the prominent St. Sebald's School in the city, was expelled for holding convictions similar to those present at the baptismal service. The convictions focused on the choice of faith as allegiance to Jesus as Lord, separated from any allegiance to the lords of city or state. This gate of the medieval walled city represents both the intolerance to new ideas within the walls and the freedom of conscience and conviction beyond them.

This double event on the same day demonstrates that the Anabaptist movement was a somewhat spontaneous, decentralized, grassroots movement happening simultaneously in various places across central Europe. There was no one strong leader who spoke up and drew followers or one key city from which it spread outwards. The Anabaptist movement was literally "all over the map" geographically and the theological convictions varied almost as much by geography, circumstance, and personality. Not unlike our own time!

Hans Denck stood in a long line of German mystics who embraced a personal encounter with the divine and a toleration of difference that seemed a few centuries ahead of his time. He was baptized as an Anabaptist in Augsburg a few months after he was expelled from Nuremberg.

500th Anniversary Part 2

That same evening in January
twenty-first, fifteen, twenty-five
one more thing happened on that day
in Nuremberg some miles away;
mingling with an artist's guild,
holding anti-establishment convictions,
and salvation with no restrictions—
for that Hans Denck was almost killed;
"True Love!"[15] he cried and on his way.

This evening of January
twenty-first, twenty, twenty-five;
five hundred years we're still alive;
we do not look like we did then:
split once, split twice, split thrice, times ten.
Will we true love and learn to thrive?

Know and Follow

The center is Christ whom no one can know unless they follow him in life, and no one may follow him unless they have first known him. Woe to the one who looks elsewhere than to this goal. For whoever thinks they belong to Christ must walk the way that Christ walked.

(Hans Denck, 1526[16])

"THIRD BAPTISM"

This is the Limmat River in downtown Zurich with the spires of the Grossmünster in the distance. In the middle of the river there used to stand a fishing platform from which a bound Felix Manz was thrown into the river and drowned. The term "Anabaptist" was a derogatory nickname given by enemies; they did not choose that name for themselves, since they did not consider infant baptism as a true baptism. In a show of anger and spite, the executioners called this his "third baptism." In another twist on a term meant to be cruel, the Anabaptists came to embrace a threefold view of baptism: Spirit, water, and blood. The baptism of blood was martyrdom.

As I stood at the side of the river, I contemplated the story of how Anna Manz had stood in the same place centuries earlier, exhorting her son Felix to be steadfast in his faith commitment. I wondered whether I might not rather say to my young adult child, "Okay, you've made your point. Stop with the drama and come home. Why do you have to go to this length?"

There is also a wonderful story about the installation of the plaque on the side of the river (close to the boat dock on the right), which I heard from our local guide, Ruedi Reich, who was part of the installation ceremony. In the 1950s when Mennonite World Conference met in Zurich, the city was approached by Mennonite leaders asking to put up this plaque. The city council flatly denied the request with the words, "We do not put up monuments to our enemies." Christendom dies hard! It seems some Reformed pastors in the city heard about this incident and decided to initiate an apology and a meeting of reconciliation. To make a long story short, in 2004 the plaque was finally unveiled with local Reformed leaders and Mennonite representatives from around the world present.

The Reformation and the Anabaptists – Steps to Reconciliation
26 June 2004, Zurich, Switzerland

INAUGURATION OF THE MEMORIAL PLAQUE TO THE
"Anabaptist Martyrs of Zurich"

Rev. Ruedi Reich, President of the Council
of the Evangelical-reformed Church of the Canton of Zurich

Dear sisters and brothers,

We commemorate here our brothers in Christ who were cruelly tortured and executed for their faith during the Reformation. The Reformation in Zurich regarded itself as a rediscovery of the liberating Gospel of Jesus Christ. For this, the members of the newly forming protestant Church were also ready to give up their lives.

We are therefore all the more ashamed and pained that the Reformed Church should have become a persecutor. In the Zurich of the Reformation, our brothers in the faith of anabaptist convictions were persecuted, tortured and cruelly executed in a combined action by Church and State. We acknowledge this historic sin and, from today's point of view, consider it a betrayal of the Gospel. Before God and before men, we point to this dark side of the Reformation, and we ask God and you, dear brothers and sisters of the Mennonite faith, to forgive us. We are grateful for the fellowship with the Mennonites in the past and today. In the midst of a violent world, we wish to work together for peace, reconciliation and justice. May this reconciliation with each other give us the strength to work together commissioned by Jesus Christ as agents of reconciliation, in small things and in great ones. For this, we ask God's blessing with all our heart.[17]

Last Words

Only love to God through Christ shall stand and prevail; not boasting, denouncing, or threatening. It is love alone that is pleasing to God; those that do not show love shall not stand in the sight of God. The true love of Christ shall scatter the enemy; so that the one who would be an heir with Christ is taught that they must be merciful, as the Father in Heaven is merciful.

(Felix Manz, 1526[18])

"CHAINS"

Many Anabaptists were imprisoned and martyred for their independent and rebellious faith because it threatened the status quo of the time—a system that depended on loyalty to both church and state. It threatened not only sacramental theology but the very economic and political stability of the times.

This particular set of chains is in a tower of Thun Castle in Switzerland where Anabaptists were imprisoned.

The frame is made from old rusty nails that represent the nails that crucified Jesus Christ. Anabaptists saw their imprisonment and martyrdom as participating in the death of Christ. They reasoned that if Jesus, their Lord and Savior, was persecuted and killed for his radical faith stance against the principalities and powers of his day, then his followers should not expect to be treated any differently! In fact, they were humbled and honored to share in the same fate. The matte of plain, hand-cut cardboard symbolizes this simple yet deep faith. *Martyrs' Mirror* recounts many stories of how Anabaptists gladly accepted the ultimate consequences of their faith.

A Letter From Nelleken Jasper

Warm greetings to you all, my dear sisters and brothers in the Lord. My friends, you need to know that I am happy and doing well. My mind has not changed, and I will continue to stick to the eternal truth till my dying breath.

Let me tell you what happened to me. I was brought before the leaders. There were four of them: the governor, two judges, and the clerk of the court. When I came into the room, I bowed to them and the governor said, "Well, my daughter, how are you?" I replied, "Quite well sir." He asked me if I was not tired of sitting in jail here and I said, "Yes, I am, why don't you do away with me sooner rather than later. You've killed my parents and my two friends, and I miss them very much." The governor said, "Don't talk like this, my child. Give up your stubborn opinions and you can go free. It would make me too sad to do this to you. You haven't been baptized; you have no reason to be here. Give it up!"

The judge asked the governor, "She has not yet been baptized?" "No," I said, "I have not been baptized, but if you released me tonight, I would be baptized by tomorrow, I promise you!" Then they sighed over me, and I said, "The two boys were not baptized." They replied, "That is true; we tried to change their opinions, but they would not budge." And I said, "I won't leave my faith commitment either!" They warned me that I could suffer the same fate, and I said, "Go ahead, roast me on a rotisserie, boil me in oil, I will continue to trust that God's grace will keep me in his truth till my dying breath. You might as well do it today rather than wait till tomorrow."

I firmly trust in God that he will help me. I have fixed my confidence in the Word, where it says, "Oh my chosen, do not be afraid; I will protect you in fire and in water, and I will not allow you to be tempted above what you are able to bear."

Then they said, "Daughter, you've been deceived, your parents led you astray; you were only a child and they had authority over you; and you in your innocence followed them. Now you have grown up a little and are out from under their influence. Surely you have the ability to make up your own mind. Give up your silly opinions and the king will pardon you. You are young yet. You are beautiful. You could get married to a fine young man."

I said that I surely have my own mind and that I would rather keep what I have in the present. They said I should take some time to think about it and I said that I had thought about it

enough already and wasn't about to change for their sake. They tried another approach. "What about your soul? Don't you want to be saved and go to heaven?" I told them that many people just wanted an easy ticket to heaven, but that few were willing to suffer with Christ. They argued that being a Christian had little to do with suffering. I said, "Christ himself had to suffer, how much more do we?" but they did not reply to this and instead said that I could talk to some priests about it. I said I wasn't interested in this; that I wanted to keep what I had. They said, "If you died tonight, you would go straight to hell. Your parents and your two friends would be glad to be in your place, to have another chance to change their minds." I said that I knew better than that!

We talked and argued a lot more, but it would take me too long to write it all, and besides, I've forgotten much of it. So, my dear friends, whom I love from my deepest heart, please pray for me that I will be able to end my life to the praise of God.

Dear friends, I have to be honest with you, I still may have to go through a great desert and sometimes I am very scared. This is a lonely and dangerous place. It's like walking through thistles and thorns. But I also know that a crown of life is prepared for us. We have the eternal truth, and I don't think any other will ever be found. God is a faithful supporter, a strength in weakness and a comforter in sad times. Let us snuggle close in God's arms and throw all our anxieties on God for God cares for us and will watch over us. One day we will all be together sitting around the table in heaven.

And so I commend you to the Lord, to the mighty word of grace. May the peace of God rule in your hearts. Say hi to all my friends.

Sincerely, Nelleken Jasper, a girl from Blijenburg, your unworthy sister in the Lord, December 12, 1569.

P.S. Please write back. I would love to get a letter sometime.[19]

"THE ROAD TO SCHLEITHEIM"

It is hard to develop a theology when you are constantly on the run and fearing for your life! The Schleitheim Confession was the first attempt to articulate essential Anabaptist beliefs and practices. The unique thing about the confession is that it is more about how to live and practice church than it is about what to believe. Does this mean that the Anabaptists just accepted the previous creeds on beliefs about God and salvation, or was this confession saying that how one lives and practices church are really more important than carefully articulated theology?

The building where the Schleitheim Confession was debated, discussed, and eventually written does not exist anymore. It could have been a private house or even a barn. Representatives from various congregations and different walks of life, from both Switzerland and southern Germany, came to a specified secret location; it was not a publicized conference of theological elites who hammered out the first Anabaptist confession.

There is a monument up in the hills close to a possible location of this meeting and the way there is not accessible by motor coach, so a local farmer took us up by tractor and wagon. This was closer to the way the first pilgrims would have made their way to this historic meeting.

Schleitheim

We travel on a road
we do not know
to a border-town
we do not know
but we will meet
and come to know
what we believe together.

We travel on a road
we do not know
to a Lord and Saviour
whom we long to know
and we will meet
and come to know
each other in his name.

We return on a road
we do not know
to a destination
we do not know
but we trust in Jesus
whom we'll come to know
in glory by and by.

The Schleitheim Confession

(Much Abridged Modern Version[20])

Baptism is a choice to follow Jesus.
Be accountable to each other.
Eating together is a sign of unity.
Be counter-cultural in your lifestyle.
Gatherings should have a leader.
Don't kill or harm anyone.
Keep your speech simple.

"CASTLE CHURCH"

I have never visited Münichau Castle where Helena von Freyburg lived and hosted an Anabaptist congregation. In fact, to my knowledge, it has never been on the itinerary of any Anabaptist heritage tour. I recently discovered that not only does this castle still exist, but it has been remodeled into a very nice hotel open to the public. Why has it not been on any itinerary? Why do von Freyburg and other women get so scant attention in Anabaptist history books when women had a prominent role in Anabaptist origins? Perhaps it is the lingering patriarchal bias in our western society. To attempt to correct this imbalance in a small way, I have included this painting of the hotel and her story in the collection, and I will make sure that if I ever lead another Anabaptist Heritage Tour, it will be on the itinerary!

Helena von Freyburg was exposed to Anabaptism probably in late 1527 and was baptized in March 1528, perhaps at the same occasion as a more well-known Anabaptist leader, Pilgram Marpeck. The two of them were prominent members of the same congregation in Rattenberg for a time and worked together on some projects, although neither was the pastor.

Soon after her baptism, Helena von Freyburg made the castle where she lived a center for Anabaptist activity. She visited Anabaptist prisoners, provided financial support, led Bible studies, and was an intermediary between Anabaptist preachers and the nobility. In 1529 a warrant for her arrest was made and she fled to Constance, returning home some years later at the request of her family. According to her confession, it seems that she made a forced recantation of her faith to do this, but then deeply regretted it. Her husband, who was not an Anabaptist, died in 1538; it seems after that she continued her ministries of teaching and advocacy with increasing boldness until her death in 1545.

Anneken Jans

I hear the trumpet sounding
God calls me to obey
Is it David Joris
holding power and sway
or can I speak?

I hear the trumpet sounding
I want to lend my voice
To what lengths must I go
to be heard above the noise
of wars and men?[21]

The Role of Women

It is significant that the concept of the priesthood of all believers among Anabaptists elevated women to a role of partnership in the congregation of believers. In the state churches, Catholic and Protestant, the attitude toward women was as yet quite medieval and remained so for many years. However, in Anabaptist circles women were referred to as sisters, and were held in the highest respect. The freedom with which they lived and associated with the men in the work of the church accounts for the incorrect and slanderous charge made by the opponents that the Anabaptists had their women in common… Anabaptist women were not a bit behind the Anabaptist men in understanding the interpretation of the gospel or in steadfast suffering for the truth of Christ.

(Myron Augsburger, 1978[22])

"JACOB HUTTER'S PRISON"

Jacob Hutter was imprisoned in this tower in the courtyard of Emperor Maximilian in the city of Innsbruck, Austria. Towers, sometimes even cathedral towers, made effective prisons because if someone attempted escape, they could fall to their death or at least experience incapacitating injury! Hutter was kept here in waiting for his execution, which happened directly below in the public square. The methods of his torture and execution were particularly brutal. To me, it felt very uncomfortable to think that I, along with hundreds of tourists in the courtyard, was trampling on Hutter's ashes.

Jacob Hutter was not the founder of the Hutterites, but he was instrumental in guiding them and organizing them in a time of upheaval and division. Thus, it is appropriate that his name carries on. During his life he traveled back and forth between his home in Innsbruck and the Anabaptist communities in Moravia.

As one who grew up on the Canadian prairies, I was familiar with Hutterites as communal farmers not far from my own family farm. However, I had no idea at the time that they were my spiritual cousins with the same roots in the Anabaptist movement of the 16th century. In my studies in college and seminary, I was very surprised to learn that they were of the most effective Anabaptist evangelists of the late 16th and early 17th century! I was also surprised to learn about the deep mystical spirituality of this branch of the Anabaptists.

The Execution of Jacob Hutter

Hat maker
up in the tower
dining with rats
not making hats.

"Silence the voice
that says faith's a choice!
Bring him down,
middle of town!
Whip him bloody,
sting with whiskey!
Freeze him cold
for being bold!"

Tongues of fire.
Funeral pyre.
Under the golden roof
they watched it all.
Under the golden roof
they saw him fall.
Now it's a mall—
and we're trampling
on his ashes.

Love Is Like Fire

Love is like fire –
When it is first kindled in a person,
small troubles and temptations smother
and hinder it; but when it really burns,
having kindled the person's eagerness for God,
the more temptations and tribulations meet it,
the more it flares, until it overcomes and consumes
all injustice and wickedness.

(Peter Riedemann, Hutterite pastor and writer, 1532[23])

"EASTER WORSHIP SERVICE"

In this house in Augsburg, Germany, Susanna Daucher hosted 88 Anabaptist believers for an Easter sunrise worship service on April 12, 1528. The reason Anabaptists came to Augsburg is because it was a relatively safe city for various reforming groups—although it came to be dominated by Lutherans. Unfortunately, for this Anabaptist group, it became dangerous. They were discovered by the authorities and all participants were arrested for this illegal activity. Some were later released while others were eventually imprisoned or executed.

As an Anabaptist historian I was quite excited to be part of the first North American group of pilgrims to discover the plaque on the side of this house on an inconspicuous street corner in the city. We had received information that the plaque had been put up a few months before, on the 485th anniversary of the event in 2013. But because of its recent placement, we did not know the exact location and very few locals knew about it, thus we had an adventure trying to find it!

It was common for early Anabaptist worship services to be held in secret hard-to-find places, because they were considered a threat to religious and political stability. In addition to urban homes of the sympathetic such as this, Anabaptist meetings also took place in more remote areas in caves and barns.

Ode to Augsburg

Augsburg deserves an ode.
It's on the old Roman military road.
Named after the emperor, a Caesar—
the same one when Jesus was born.
"Peace on earth, good will toward men!"
Augsburg, O Augsburg, bring us that peace!
Augsburg: a free imperial city
Augsburg: a free Protestant city
Augsburg: a free capitalist city with
Bankers, Fuggers, Welsers, Hochstetters—
all money makers.
Augsburg brought some of that peace—
they built Europe's first social housing project!

Augsburg, O Augsburg, bring us the peace
and let the Anabaptists in to the feast.
In Augsburg Hans Denck was baptized, fifteen-twenty-six
and he baptized others including Hans Hut.
But—then they found themselves in a fix
at a meeting discussing eschatology and theology with no frivolity!
After that meeting in fifteen-twenty-seven,
some went to heaven
earlier than they counted on,
which is why it's now called the Synod of the Martyrs!
Augsburg, O Augsburg, bring us peace, not horrors.
But then Helene von Freyburg found refuge here
And Pilgram Marpeck moved here
because he was an engineer.
Augsburg was a place of peace; they had no fear!

Augsburg, O Augsburg, you saw so much war and strife
but finally made the peace in fifteen-fifty-five.
"You can be a Lutheran.
You can be a Catholic.
Freedom of religion.
We want you all to thrive!"
The Peace of Augsburg was good
until war broke out again… and again,
and the Anabaptists had all fled to Moravia.
Augsburg, O Augsburg, bring us peace again.

Cave Worship Service

Today we parked at a farm in the Emmental Valley in Switzerland and hiked to a hidden cave in the forested hills where Anabaptists secretly held worship services in the 17th century. Water from a spring dripped down in a gentle waterfall above our heads as we prayed, read Scripture, sang a song, and shared communion together. It was a very moving experience to imagine having to do this many years ago, knowing we might be in trouble if discovered. It was quite surreal until a fighter jet screamed overhead in the middle of the service, adding a disturbing layer to my imagination exercise! It made me wonder whether I would have had the courage to attend this worship service if I had known we were in danger of being bombed had we been discovered. I gained a new respect for my spiritual ancestors who fled to this remote area from the cities because of persecution. It seems Mennonites didn't become farmers out of choice but out of survival.

As we visit here on a tour as modern pilgrims, I sometimes wonder if we are losing what these people died for. They were persecuted because they believed that faith transcended political boundaries and familial connections. This was a threat to the status quo of that era. As we travel across Europe finding family names on tombstones and visiting beautiful cathedrals where faith seems to have become a cultural relic of the past, it has reminded me that Anabaptism is not kept alive by monuments, "Mennonite names," and nostalgic feelings, but by a radical and communal faith that declares allegiance to the Prince of Peace alone despite the threats of other gods in our western society.[24]

"MENNO'S FIRST CHURCH"

Menno Simons was probably trained in a Franciscan monastery not far from his home and became a simple country priest in this church building in his hometown of Pingjum, Friesland, in the Netherlands. By all accounts he was not an exceptional priest and he confessed that he spent too much of his time in idleness, playing cards and drinking wine.

Menno did receive a copy of the Scriptures, which he began to earnestly read and study, eventually finding out that he had been deceived on a number of matters, including baptism, communion, and the use of the sword. It took him more than a decade after this to finally leave the Catholic Church. Was it due to his slow and deliberate Frisian nature? Was it his careful and methodical personality? Was it the influence of his countryman, Erasmus, who stayed loyal to the church while still being critical?

Although Menno became the primary pastor and apostle of the 16th-century Dutch Anabaptists and wrote more than any other Anabaptist of his era, I still see him as an ordinary rural pastor on a first-name basis with his parishioners: unpretentious, plain, measured, vulnerable, and caring. This simple brown brick building behind layers of hand-cut matte without a glass protection are meant to symbolize those qualities, as if you could reach out and touch him and get to know him as a brother in Christ. Most other leaders in history are known by their last name; he is always known as "Menno."

The Confession of Menno Simons

I sat in my parish, wiled time away
No direction, no Scripture to guide me
Idleness, wine-drinking, cards did I play
What is my future? What will I be?

Doubts haunt me about the wine and the bread
I heard of ten baptized, killed for their stand
Then I got a Bible that no one had read
I search for the faithful, I must join that band

In Munster, these rebaptizers confuse
Jan Van Leiden you blasphemer! I wrote
With violence, they wait for God to diffuse
The pope's army with more violence doth smote

The blood of these sheep fell so hot on my heart
I surrender to thee, my saviour thou art.

Menno Hears My Confession

Menno, I love thee more than words can tell
Your sin-cer-i-ty and sim-pli-ci-ty
I love your deep eyes and your beard as well
Your pastoral heart for the community

But oh dear Menno, the ban went too far
Strict Frisian nature got the best of you then
Schisms, secessions, oh look at the scar
Let me hide in my contemplative den

And Menno, what of the celestial flesh?
Your quest for purity has got out of hand
Five hundred years later we pray, we wish
For some unity in Mennonite land

And, oh dear Menno, let me be a bard
I like my occasional wine and cards!

"THE CAGES OF MÜNSTER"

The Münster Anabaptists had a vision of a peaceable Christian kingdom, but they believed that it should be set up by using violent force. When an Anabaptist faction won an election in the city, they forced residents to be re-baptized and to live communally, instituting various Old Testament practices in literal fashion, including polygamy. Their leaders declared themselves prophets and kings; and, when the occupying Christian empire put down the rebellion with greater force and violence, they were executed and hung in these cages on the tower of St. Lambert's Church as an example for the populace of what happens to radicals. The cages were taken down in the 20th century when repairs were made to the church building, but they were put back up as a continuing reminder.

I was not expecting my emotional reaction upon visiting Münster. It was a miserably cold day in May with a driving rain; and as I gazed up at the cages my tears mixed with the rain for the brutal cycle of violence done in the name of Christ.

The Münster debacle was a tragic and terrible event that illustrates the extremes of the Anabaptist movement. Although it was very much on the fringes of Anabaptism, it was very influential in shaping the theology and practice of Anabaptists for generations to come. Münster was a defining moment even if it was something to react against. Menno Simons' first essay as a priest was entitled "The Blasphemies of Jan Van Leiden" (who was a leader in Münster). It is ironic that Menno later joined the movement, albeit he sought to distance himself from the ideologies of Münster. He and most Mennonites after him have seen pacifism as central to the Gospel.

The Sad Saga of Münster

War. It rages, rages, rages.
In the Bible's pages.
It started with Cain.
Joshua killed the Canaanites.
David killed the Amorites.
The bloody stain.
God has commanded it; evil must be eradicated!
Enemies must be subjugated!

War. It rages, rages, rages.
In history's pages.
Israel versus Palestine
Muslim versus Jew, and Christians too
Protestant versus Catholic
Orthodox versus Orthodox; Russia versus Ukraine
The bullets rain.
War. It rages, rages, rages.
Even Anabaptists 500 years ago.
Say it ain't so!

It was so, in Münster—city of churches.
What better place to proclaim:
"Get ready, Jesus is coming again!
The world is coming to a refrain!
Come to the city of churches to be saved!
Bring the blind and bring the lame!
Jesus is coming again!"
And so they came!

This is how it happened.

Jan the Baker from Haarlem met Jan the Bueker from Leiden.
Jan from Haarlem baptized Jan from Leiden.
Jan from Haarlem went to Amsterdam where he left his wife and found a queen.
He gave a damn to some and love to some and said he was a king.
And then he baptized and he baptized and he baptized and he baptized—
until he reached 144 thousand.
Bernhard Rothmann, the theologian, was one of them.
He was the man in Münster.
Let's be Anabaptists. Let us sing.

"Come to Münster! Come to the city of churches! Come to the city of God!
Save yourselves from the corrupt generation!
Come to Münster for your salvation!"
And they came.

Münster the city of churches. Münster the city of God.
Münster the city of refuge. Münster the city of peace.
Only the pure and baptized shall abide.
Everyone who dared resist—they died.
By the hand of God administered by the hand of man, Jan the Bakerman.

"Come to Münster! Come to the city of churches! Come to the city of God!
Judgment day will come on the day of resurrection.
Save yourselves from the corrupt generation!
Come to Münster for your salvation!"

They came from south in Strasbourg.
They came from north by sea.
They came from east in Holland.
They came from Westphalie.
They came.

And Easter came.
And it *was* judgment day.
For Jan the Baker.
He was toast.

So Jan from Leiden took control. God told him so.
And the Bible told him what to do.
Share your goods and take more wives.
And those who didn't lost their lives.
Including some of Jan from Leiden's wives.

Jan from Leiden was the king. God told him so.
You dare not sing—a protest song.
When one of his wives dared to sing, he said,
"Off with your head! You're better off dead!"
Then in front of the rest he trampled her body.
Such dread!

"Come to Münster! Come to the city of churches! Come to the city of God!"
Some tried. Some died.
Then suddenly the coming stopped.

The Bishop and his army in the name of Christ.
They sieged the city. They starved them out.
These bloody Anabaptists!
Their blood will flow!
And for two days their blood did flow.
And then it was quiet.
No more to and fro.

Münster the city of churches. Münster the city of God.
Münster the city of refuge. Münster the city of peace.

Jan from Leiden, now king in disgrace.
He and his council were tortured and tried.
Their bodies were pinched and pierced and fried,
ripped and burned and stabbed, until they died.
Then hung in cages from the cathedral spire.
Then hung in cages from the cathedral spire.
Then hung in cages from the cathedral spire.

"This is what happens to revolutionaries! Let this be a warning!"
The cages are still there,
hanging from the cathedral spire.

Oh! The cages, the cages, the cages
The battle still rages, and rages, and rages
It was so long, so long ago, so long
They were so wrong, so wrong, so wrong
But still when men are wrong we kill, we kill, we kill
With guns or words or otherwise… reprise
We do not learn from history
Instead, instead repeat, instead repeat it.

"MENNO'S MOTTO"

Ten days after the Münster debacle ended, Menno left the priesthood and joined the Anabaptists. "The blood of these misguided sheep fell so hot on my heart that I could not stand it!"[25] He became the apostle to this fledgling new movement.

On the title page of everything Menno Simons wrote is 1 Corinthians 3:11. "For no other foundation can anyone lay except that which is laid, which is Jesus Christ." This verse has become indicative of subsequent Anabaptist/Mennonite theology that emphasizes that the Christian life is primarily about following Jesus, and that reading the Bible should be done with a "Christo-centric" lens.

The writing on the actual monument is in Dutch and describes the site near Witmarsum, Netherlands as the place where Menno preached his first "evangelical" sermon, meaning that the sermon was based on the Bible rather than simply reading a previous sermon approved by the church authorities. I have simplified the inscription by just rendering his motto Bible verse in English. The Bible verse appears in Dutch on the monument in the background.

1 Corinthians 3:11 has since become the motto verse of Mennonite Church Canada and inspired the name of Meserete Kristos (Foundation Jesus Christ), an Ethiopian Mennonite denomination.

Roll Over Menno

(A sermon based on 1 Corinthians 3:1-23)

In 1956, Chuck Berry wrote and recorded one of the early rock 'n roll songs entitled "Roll over Beethoven, dig these rhythm and blues…" The basic message of the song was that if Beethoven knew the kind of music that was being popularized, he might "roll over in his grave." But it was also hoped that Beethoven might be rolling over in his grave to tap his toes and dance—he might be surprised that he would "dig" or approve of the music.

The same might also be true for Menno Simons if he knew what was all happening in his name! He would probably not be surprised that there was a church named after him, because even in his day, people who were part of one of the churches he pastored in the coastal areas of northern Europe were nicknamed "Mennists" and later "Mennonites."

Menno probably would be surprised that in a few centuries after his death there would be more Mennonites in every other continent than in his homeland of Europe (not counting Australia). But I think he would probably "dig" this! In fact, there are now more of Menno's spiritual offspring in Africa than there are in North America!

Menno might be rolling over in his grave with anguish and disappointment when it comes to some other aspects of Mennonite history. Those who go by the name of Menno have seen much division and separation. Although Anabaptists were persecuted mercilessly by both Catholics and Protestants in the 16th century, we already had internal schisms between Swiss/German Anabaptists and Dutch Mennonites over Christology and church discipline. Then in 1693 the Amish broke away from other Swiss/German Anabaptists over issues of worldliness and church discipline. In 1812 the Kleinegemeinde (small church) broke away from the Grosse Gemeinde (large church) in Russia over similar issues. This was followed in 1860 by the secession of the Mennonite Brethren. There have been many other splits and departures over

the years so that today there are more than two dozen different Mennonite denominations in North America alone.

1 Corinthians 3 would seem to indicate that the Corinthians had some similar problems two thousand years ago. The Corinthians were also divided. They lined up behind their favorite leaders: "Have you heard Apollos? He is an amazing speaker, let's go to his church." "Well, he may be young and exciting, but you can't replace the solid biblical preaching of Paul." "Oh, but don't forget Peter, now he has all the tools!" And on it went. The Corinthians were comparing, quarreling, and jealously jumping from one bandwagon to the next.

It is easy for us to criticize the Corinthian church but maybe we still have some of the same problems today. What about (insert your church name) today? Perhaps we are tempted to split and splinter like the Corinthians and Mennonites of the past. The pandemic does not seem to have helped church unity or attendance. I have observed four theological directions among Mennonites in Canada, based on John Roth's insightful analysis of Mennonites in the USA.[26] All four directions are rooted in Scripture and all of them can make a legitimate claim to being rooted in 16th-century Anabaptism, although I'm sure most believe that their particular one is the most faithful!

Very briefly: "Evangelical Anabaptism" emphasizes the centrality and authority of Scripture as well as the importance of the new birth and a radically transformed life of discipleship. "Spiritual Anabaptism" emphasizes openness to the Spirit and openness of expression with two distinct expressions I call "charismatic" and "contemplative." "Progressive Anabaptism" seeks to engage the powers on the issues of our day: racial reconciliation, inclusion of the marginalized, economic justice, and nonviolent peacemaking. "Separatist Anabaptism" seeks to be separated from the evils of the world ethically, culturally, and geographically. We might be able to label ourselves or others as tending toward one of these directions, but the point is that we find ourselves in the same splintered situation as the Corinthians!

Now listen to what Paul says to the Corinthians, because it might have some relevance for us. Paul uses two analogies to drive home his point. In agriculture there are people engaged in different activities that all contribute: one plants, another waters, others add fertilizer, some prune, others harvest—but it is God who makes things grow. When building a house there are many subcontractors: one pours the basement, another raises the walls; there are roofers, dry-wallers, electricians, plumbers, painters, and finishers. Each one works with different materials, but each one is needed. In the end it is God who works in human lives.

The reality is that each one—Peter, Paul, Apollos, and others—still had to be faithful to

who God was calling them to be. It is true that Anabaptist origins can be described as polygenesis or having multiple beginnings. We should understand then that this might result in a variety of equally valid contemporary expressions. We need the evangelical, Bible-based, born-again, holy-living among us. We need the Spirit-filled, hand-raising, mystical, meditating as part of our community. We need the progressive, inclusive, social-justice active to speak up in our midst. We need the conservative, wary-of-the-world to warn us rather than leave us.

Then comes Paul's punchline in the central and climactic verse 11. It is the hub of the spokes that make the wheel strong and able to turn. It is notable that this became Menno Simons' motto verse. "For no one can lay any foundation other than the one that is laid, which is Jesus Christ." On every single piece of his published writing Menno always had this verse at the beginning. Did you know that one of the largest Mennonite denominations in the world, Meserite Kristos in Ethiopia, is also named after this verse? Their name translated is "Foundation Jesus Christ."

Is Menno rolling over in his grave when we exacerbate our differences? What does this motto verse mean for us today? What does it mean to have Jesus Christ as our church foundation? Of course, everyone in the world who identifies with the name of Jesus would claim to hold Jesus as the center, but I want to look uniquely at how Anabaptist/Mennonites see it, using the outline from Palmer Becker's book, *Anabaptist Essentials*.[27]

The person of Jesus is foundational for our faith. The key phrase for Anabaptist/Mennonites is not *faith in Jesus* but *following Jesus in faith*. To make Jesus foundational means more than just believing that Jesus died for us and takes away our sin in a spiritual way and promises eternal life. Jesus' kingdom is not merely in a spiritual dimension—somewhere we go when we die—it is right here and right now. It matters how I live my life every day. I attempt to follow the ways and teachings of Jesus in my daily life. The fact that Jesus was who he claimed to be, God in the flesh, is central to how we read the Bible and how we live. The things that Jesus taught and exemplified in his life: compassion, forgiveness, acceptance, justice for the oppressed are values we incorporate into our lives.

The community of Jesus is central to our life. We follow Jesus in community. Believer's Baptism incorporates people into the body of Christ, the church. We are called to commit ourselves not only to Christ but to the body of Christ. True community takes work—and grace—to embrace those who are different, and to listen to those who think differently. Jesus is the central magnet of our communities of faith. If we are drawn closer to our center, we draw closer to each other and we don't need to focus so much on making or defending boundaries.

Thirdly, the way of Jesus is central to our work. The way of Jesus is the way of the cross. The way of the cross is the way of love and peace. The ruling powers of our society operate in the way of terrorism and counterterrorism, violence and counter-violence. "If you kill our people, we will kill more of yours." The way of Jesus is the opposite. The way of the cross seems foolish in light of these horrors, and yet that is what we are called to. The way of love dispels fear and terror, and the way of peace deals a death blow to enmity and violence. The way of reconciliation brings enemies together. How can we witness to the way of love and peace in the world if we can't even live with evangelicals, progressives, charismatics/contemplatives, and conservatives in the same church or denomination? Rhetorical question!

Roll over Menno. Do you dig this? We don't follow Paul or Peter or Apollos or Priscilla and Aquilla. We don't follow *(insert the names of your favorite Mennonite leaders of the present)*. We are not in competition between evangelicals, progressives, charismatics/contemplatives, and conservatives. We're on the same team. Jesus is our foundation. We follow Jesus in community, doing the work of reconciliation.

"STRASBOURG"

This picture is of the Rosetta window in the main cathedral of Strasbourg, France. Strasbourg was a progressive city during the Reformation that welcomed a free exchange of goods as well as ideas. Almost every Anabaptist leader of note was in the city at one time or another. Many sought refuge, others became prominent civic employees (Pilgram Marpeck), some came to learn, and still others came to preach. Melchior Hoffman picked up some Anabaptist ideas here from Swiss and German brothers and sisters who were present and took them back to his Dutch homeland, forming a unique branch of the Anabaptist movement. Strasbourg was an important city for the Anabaptists.

For a time in the 20th century, Mennonite World Conference appropriately had their head offices in the city. The colorful, round Rosetta window symbolizes for us both the safety which many Anabaptists of the 16th century found and also the varied global expressions of Anabaptism today.

Today, the Anabaptist movement has followers on every inhabited continent. Ironically, every continent (other than Australia) has more Anabaptists than Europe, where it originated. The Anabaptist movement that began with a few fledgling fellowships has grown into thousands of congregations with over two million participants in more than eighty countries.

A global Anabaptist assembly took place in Strasbourg in 1984. Since then, assemblies have been held in Canada, India, Zimbabwe, Paraguay, USA, and Indonesia.

I Was There

I was there in Winnipeg in 1990
when ten thousand Mennonites from around the world
descended on a city that already had ten thousand
and another ten thousand in the surrounding area
who all thought they were the true remnant
but when I was there,
I began to realize how small my view of the church was.

Before I was there
I used to think Mennonites were like manure—
it helps to fertilize the soil if spread out evenly,
but it really stinks if left in one pile for a long time
but this time when they gathered in one big pile
it was like fine perfume wafting up in the rafters of an old hockey arena
and I was there
to smell it (with apologies to those who were allergic to strong scents).

I was there when all thirty thousand gathered
on Sunday in the open-air
with the African choir
and the Asian dancers
and the Latinx preacher
and we had sweet communion
with awkward prepackaged wafers and sealed containers of grape juice;
it was a long three-hour moment
with everything said and sung in four or more languages,
but it seemed so short
because it was a foretaste of the heavenly banquet
I will never forget because
I was there.

Perspective From the Global South

Although history is the narrative of past events, its primary goal is to help those concerned to come to a better knowledge of their identity. While helping us take a retrospective look at past events, history also invites us to learn the lessons of our strengths and weaknesses in order to better handle the present and to plan for the future.

As Mennonites and Brethren in Christ we have a heritage that must be preserved and transmitted to all those with whom we have contact. As part of the Reformation, the Anabaptists conformed their lives to the teachings of Scriptures. This return to the Word of truth allowed them to forge an identity founded on biblical values that they transmitted from generation to generation to their descendants.

Historically, Mennonite and Brethren in Christ churches are known as peace churches. This particularity has been the strength of Anabaptist descendants in history and is still necessary today. The entire world is sick because of wars and rumours of war. Everywhere peace is fragile. Churches [with an Anabaptist heritage] must be actively engaged in fostering a culture of peace.

(Siaka Traore, Mennonite pastor and theologian, Burkina Faso, 2006[28])

Anabaptist Origins Timeline

1522

February — Andreas Castelberger organizes a Bible study group that came to be nicknamed the "School of Heretics."

March — A group of people gathers at the home of Christopher Froschauer, breaking Lent by eating sausage!

Wilhelm Reublin is expelled from Zurich for his critique of the Mass.

1523

January 29 — First Zurich disputation where Ulrich Zwingli breaks with Rome.

April 18 — Wilhelm Reublin marries Adelheid Leeman becoming the first priest to do so in Switzerland.

September — Hans Denck becomes rector of St. Sebald's School in Nuremburg.

Fall — Tithe, Mass, and Iconoclasm controversies erupt in the Zurich region.

October 26-29 — Second Zurich Disputation focuses on authority of Scripture, the Mass, church relationship to state, etc.

1524

March 26 — Menno Simons is ordained as a priest.

Spring — Wilhelm Reublin refuses to baptize infants in Zollikon.

August — He is imprisoned for it.

September 5 — Conrad Grebel and friends write a letter to Thomas Muntzer outlining their convictions on church order, communion, the sword, etc.

October — Belthasar Hubmaier reforms preaching and communion in Waldshut.

Fall — Hans Denck is implicated in the trial of the "godless painters."

December 6 and 13 — "Tuesday Disputations" in Zurich between Zwingli and "School of Heretics" members regarding baptism.

1525

January 17	The first public disputation in Zurich focused on baptism.
January 21	Grebel baptizes George Blaurock; he in turn baptizes others who are gathered in the home of Felix Manz in Zurich.
January 21	Denck is expelled from Nuremburg for convictions like those of the circle in Zurich.
January 29	Manz and Blaurock are arrested and released soon after.
March 25	Blaurock is banished from Zurich.
April 9 (Palm Sunday[29])	Grebel baptizes several hundred people in St. Gallen.
April 16 (Easter)	Reublin baptizes Hubmaier in Waldshut who in turn baptizes 300 in the next month.
May 15	The slaughter of 6,000 peasants at Frankenhausen in the Peasants' War. Some survivors, like Hans Hut, become Anabaptists.
May 29	Eberli Bolt becomes first known Anabaptist martyr.
Summer	Anabaptism spreads to Basel, Bern, Lucerne, and other Swiss cities.
July 27	Hans Krusi burned at the stake to become the second Anabaptist martyr.
September	Denck arrives in Augsburg and is baptized by Hubmaier.
October 8	Grebel is arrested.
November 6–8	Formal disputation regarding baptism with "School of Heretics" members involved.
November 18	"School of Heretics" members, Margaret Hottinger, Michael Sattler, and others are arrested and tried.
December 5	Hubmaier is driven from Waldshut.
December 21	Hubmaier participates in a public disputation regarding baptism in Zurich.
All year	Menno Simons is "playing cards and drinking wine" as a priest's assistant in Pingjum, Holland.

1526

March 7	"School of Heretics" members receive life sentences and are imprisoned.
March 21	They escape prison.
April 15	Hubmaier writes his Confession of Faith.
July	Hubmaier arrives in Nikolsberg, Moravia; the Anabaptist community grows and is strengthened.
May 26 (Pentecost)	Denck baptizes Hans Hut.
June	Michael Sattler commits himself to Anabaptism.
Fall	Jakob Hutter purchases a New Testament in Tyrol and becomes an Anabaptist.
December 25	Denck expelled from Strasbourg after theological debates.

1527

January 5	Felix Manz is drowned in the Limmat River in Zurich, becoming the first Anabaptist martyr in Zurich.
January 25	"Elizabeth" Hut (daughter of Hans) is executed by drowning in Bavaria.
January	Denck baptizes Melchior Rinck.
February 24	A meeting of Anabaptists from Switzerland and southern Germany takes place at Schleitheim. A confession with seven articles is agreed upon and recorded.
Spring	Hut spreads Anabaptism to the area of Franconia.
May	Nikolsberg erupts with differences between Hubmaier and Hut and between "staff-bearers" and "sword-bearers."
May	Blaurock spreads Anabaptism to the Tyrol region of Austria.
May 17-21	The trial and brutal execution of Michael and Margareta Sattler.
July	Hubmaier and his wife, Elsbeth, are arrested.
August 20	Meetings take place in Augsburg to discuss eschatology, among other things. It came to be known as the Martyr's Synod because many who attended died as martyrs.
December 6	Hans Hut dies in his cell by asphyxiation.

1528

January	Pilgram Marpeck resigns his post as mining magistrate in Rattenberg, Tyrol.
March 10	Belthasar and Elsbeth Hubmaier are executed in Vienna.
March	Helena von Freyberg becomes an Anabaptist and makes her home, Münichau Castle in the Tyrol, a center for Anabaptist activity.
March	Jacob Wiedemann departs from Nikolsberg with about 200 staff-bearers. They pool all their resources on a blanket to become the first communal Anabaptists.
April 12 (Easter)	Susanna Daucher hosts an Easter worship service at her home in Augsburg; all 88 participants are arrested.
Spring	Communities of Anabaptists are established in Moravia beginning at Auspitz and Austerlitz.
Summer	Pilgram Marpeck becomes an Anabaptist and subsequently flees to Strasbourg.

1529

Spring	Peter Riedemann becomes an Anabaptist and is imprisoned for 3 years where he writes his first confession known as "Love Is Like Fire."
August	Melchior Rinck is imprisoned in Hesse where he dies many years later.
September 6	Blaurock is executed.

1530

January 2	Helena von Freyburg is arrested for her Anabaptist activities.
April 23	Melchior Hoffman is banished from Strasbourg where he had encountered Anabaptists.
June	Hoffman forms his own group of Anabaptists and baptizes 300 in Emden, Netherlands.

1531

March 20	Sikke Freerks executed in Leewarden, becoming the first Anabaptist martyr in the Netherlands.
December 5	Ten Anabaptists are executed in Amsterdam, forcing the Dutch Anabaptist movement to go underground.

1533

August 11	Schisms among communities in Moravia are confronted by the arrival of Jakob Hutter who assumes leadership to resolve the issues.

1534

February 27	The Münster debacle begins.
April 5 (Easter)	Jan Matthijs is killed on the day he predicted as Judgment Day. Jan Van Leiden takes over and declares himself king.
Fall	Anneken Jans leaves her substantial inheritance to become an Anabaptist in South Holland.

1535

March/April	The monastery at Oldecloister is taken over by Münsterites.
April 5	Menno's brother Pieter dies at Oldecloister.
June	Menno writes "The Blasphemy of Jan Van Leiden."

1536

January 20	The Münster debacle ends with the siege of Münster. Leaders are executed and hung in cages from St. Lambert's Church.
January 30	Menno leaves the priesthood and joins the Anabaptists.[30]

How I Became an Anabaptist

I grew up a prairie boy,
I grew up rural,
I grew up separate,
I grew up sheltered,
I grew up Low German,
I grew up in the church,
I grew up conservative,
I grew up evangelical,
I grew up Mennonite.

In school they called me a Nazi.
In school they called me a Croute.
In school they called me a Mennonite.
I wanted out.
All the words meant the same to me.
And it wasn't pleasant.
I did not want to be a Mennonite.
Did I know what it meant?
Not a mite!

Mennonites have bled.
Mennonites have fled.
Mennonites have become Alliance and Baptist and Pentecostal instead.
I didn't want to bleed. I couldn't flee.
There were no other churches in the community.
I had no options. I left my church. I left my parents' faith. I left my Jesus.

But Jesus did not leave me.
My parents prayed for me.
I returned to Jesus but I thought, it really bites
this thing about being Mennonite.
And I had never even heard of being Anabaptist.

I wrote this in my journal at age 16.

"Ed Wiebe [another preacher] came to see me about baptism into the Mennonite church! I told him no bloody way! I wasn't even a good Christian, and I told him that church didn't seem very attractive because many members were backslidden and it was a bit dry. He was a little hurt and asked if I needed any spiritual help. I said no even though I did at the time. I still can't stand help from preachers. I still can't understand some."

I've swallowed my words. I've swallowed my pride. My old self has died.
For 40 years now a Mennonite minister, I've been bona fide.
Now I'm one of those "hard to understand preachers!"

I chose then, and I choose now, to be called Mennonite.
My sister, she's not a Mennonite, even though she eats vereneki.
My pastor, she is a Mennonite, even though she's a Yamasaki.

How did it happen?
How did I become Anabaptist [a theological movement]?
How did I become Mennonite [a church of the movement]?

So, back to my youth; I was pretty uncouth.
I flirted with a lot of churches;
they seemed like so much more fun
than my old Mennonite one.

What a shock! What a surprise!
It was in public university that my faith had a reprise.
Christians were ridiculed as right wing republican war-mongers,
but Mennonites were known as nonviolent peacemakers.
It is an offense. It doesn't make sense.
But I had an opportunity. I shared the Jesus story. I shared my story.
My own faith came alive when I told it.
Maybe I should be more bold in telling it.

Then in my research at the library of Conrad Grebel University
(Did you know they named their university after someone who went to four universities, got kicked out of one, dropped out of another and never graduated from any of them?)
and at an evangelical seminary
and at an ecumenical seminary (too much seminary!),
I found out Anabaptists were sometimes somewhat contrary.
As one who also likes to roam
that made me feel right at home!

In 1990 my Mennonite world blew up, expanded
When 20,000 Mennos from all parts of the world descended… on Winnipeg!
We shook our leg, we ate the bread, we drank the dreg
More Mennos in Africa than Canada?!
I thought I died and went to heaven
Communion bread was multiplied without the leaven

Then in two thousand ten
There was another phenomenon
A non-Mennonite Brit named Stuart Murray wrote a book.
Who is this crook? Should we have a look?
In 2011 I went to England to have my look… in person.
"AAHH! It's a naked Anabaptist!"
Should we pass the fist… instead?
He took off our centuries' old clothes and I suppose
dressed us in those… of postmodernism.
Postmodernism? I'm scared of isms: communism, fascism, racism, sexism, materialism, capitalism…
But maybe, just maybe as he suggested
the spirit of Anabaptism
has something to say to us today
in the midst of our ism fray.
Is it a movement whose time has come?
Is Anabaptism something we can learn from?

500 years ago the Anabaptists died for the freedom to choose… their faith.
500 years ago the Anabaptists lived for the kingdom only to lose… their lives.
500 years ago the Anabaptists died for their political rebellion.
500 years ago the Anabaptists lived out their salvation…
as best as they knew how.
And now?

500 years later… What are we dying for?
500 years later… What are we living for?

BIBLIOGRAPHY
(FOR FURTHER READING)[31]

Augsburger, Myron S. *Faithful Unto Death: Fifteen Young People Who Were Not Afraid to Die for Their Faith*. Word, 1978.

_____. *The Fugitive: Menno Simons*. Herald, 2008.

_____. *Pilgrim Aflame*. Herald, 1967.

Becker, Palmer. *Anabaptist Essentials: Ten Signs of a Unique Christian Faith*. Herald, 2017.

Brandt, Gareth. "How Experiencing History Contributes to Spiritual Formation." *Mennonite Historian* 45 (December 2019), 2-4.

Braght, Thieleman J. van. Translated from the Dutch by Joseph F. Sohm. *Martyrs' Mirror*. Herald, 1977.

Checole, Alemu, et.al. *Anabaptist Songs in African Hearts*. Good Books, 2006.

Claiborne, Shane, and Chris Haw. *Jesus for President*. The Simple Way, 2008.

Driver, John. *Radical Faith: An Alternative History of the Christian Church*. Pandora, 1999.

Estep, William R. *The Anabaptist Story*. Eerdmans, 1996.

Fellman, Walter, editor. Translated by Edward J. Furcha with Ford Lewis Battles. *Selected Writings of Hans Denck*. Pickwick, 1975.

Global Anabaptist Encyclopedia Online. www.gameo.org

Goertz, Hans-Jurgen. *Profiles of Radical Reformers*. Herald, 1982.

_____. *The Anabaptists*. Routledge, 1996.

Harder, Leland, editor. *The Sources of Swiss Anabaptism: The Grebel Letters and Related Documents*. Herald, 1985.

Klaassen, Walter. *Anabaptism: Neither Catholic nor Protestant*. Pandora, 2001.

Klaassen, Walter, editor. *Anabaptism in Outline*. Herald, 1981.

Koop, Karl, editor. "Commemorating Anabaptism's 500 Years." *Vision: A Journal for Church and Theology* (Spring 2024) 3-96.

Murray, Stuart. *The Naked Anabaptist: The Bare Essentials of a Radical Faith*. Herald, 2015.

Riedemann, Peter. *Love Is Like Fire: The Confession of an Anabaptist Prisoner*. Plough, 2011.

Roth, John D. *Stories: How Mennonites Came to Be*. Herald, 2006.

Ruth, John L. *Conrad Grebel: Son of Zurich*. Herald, 1975.

Simons, Menno. Translated from the Dutch by Leonard Verduin and edited by J. C. Wenger. *The Complete Writings of Menno Simons*. Herald, 1956.

Snyder, C. Arnold. *Anabaptist History and Theology (Revised Student Edition)*. Pandora, 1997.

_____. *Following in the Footsteps of Christ: The Anabaptist Tradition*. Orbis, 2004.

Snyder, C. Arnold and Linda A. Huebert Hecht, editors. *Profiles of Anabaptist Women*. Wilfrid Laurier University, 1996.

Stayer, James M., Werner O. Packull and Klaus Deppermann. "From Monogenesis to Polygenesis: The Historical Discussion of Anabaptist Origins." *Mennonite Quarterly Review* 49 (April 1975): 83-121.

Weaver, J. Denny. *Becoming Anabaptist: The Origin and Significance of Sixteenth-Century Anabaptism*. Herald, 2005.

Yoder, John Howard, editor. *The Schleitheim Confession*. Herald, 1977.

ENDNOTES

[1] Much more could and should be written on this subject. See my most recent blog posts on my website at www.garethbrandt.wordpress.com (February 20 and June 21, 2023; January 18, February 28, May 15, June 21, July 25, August 12 and 17, 2022). See also recent articles: "Five Hundred Years of Anabaptism and Colonization" by Sarah Augustine and "Anabaptist Reparations after 500 Years: Mennonites and the Doctrine of Discovery" by Drew G. I. Hart, both in *Vision: A Journal for Church and Theology,* Spring 2024: 63-78.

[2] Murray, *The Naked Anabaptist,* 15.

[3] Ibid., 38.

[4] Goertz, *The Anabaptists,* 1-5.

[5] The first modern scholarly recognition of this came with the groundbreaking article, "From Monogenesis to Polygenesis" by Stayer, Packull, and Deppermann in *Mennonite Quarterly Review* in 1975.

[6] *Webster's New Explorer Dictionary*, Miriam-Webster, 1999.

[7] For an overview of some radical movements in Christian history see John Driver, *Radical Faith.*

[8] Weaver, *Becoming Anabaptist,* 9.

[9] My experiences have been with Tourmagination (www.tourmagination.com). For my account of how experiencing history has been spiritually transformative for me, see my article, "How Experiencing History Contributes to Spiritual Formation" in *Mennonite Historian,* December 2019.

[10] Ruth, *Conrad Grebel,* 148-149, 151.

[11] The inspiration and some of the quotes for this section were provided by John Driver's *Radical Faith* and *Jesus for President* by Shane Claiborne and Chris Haw.

[12] *The Complete Writings of Menno Simons,* 241-242.

[13] From *The Sources of Swiss Anabaptism: The Grebel Letters and Related Documents,* edited by Leland Harder, 301-303.

[14] The account I read was from John Ruth's book, *Conrad Grebel: Son of Zurich,* 103-106. His well-written story is based on the oldest known account of this incident in the Hutterite Chronicle.

[15] One of Hans Denck's best known writings is entitled, "Concerning True Love" in which he articulates his Anabaptist convictions around the central motif of divine love.

[16] Fellman, *Selected Writings of Hans Denck,* 46.

[17] This letter was obtained from the late Rev. Ruedi Reich in May of 2007 when he told us the story about the installation of the plaque.

[18] Braght, *Martyrs' Mirror,* 451.

[19] My edited paraphrase of a letter in *Martyrs' Mirror,* 762 was inspired by Myron Augsburger's accounts of young martyrs in *Faithful Unto Death.* For Nelleken Jasper's story see p. 50-57.

[20] For the real thing see *The Schleitheim Confession,* translated by J. H. Yoder.

[21] Aneken Jans was a poet and friend of David Joris who took her own path of nonviolent resistance, diverging from both David Joris' spiritualism and Munster's violent apocalypticism. She wrote a hymn entitled, "I Can Hear the Trumpet Sounding." Aneken Jans became an Anabaptist martyr in 1539. See J. Denny Weaver, *Becoming Anabaptist,* 139-140. For more women's stories in the Anabaptist movement read Snyder and Hecht, editors, *Profiles of Anabaptist Women.*

[22] Augsburger, *Faithful Unto Death,* 75.

[23] This is from Riedemann's shorter confession; he also wrote a longer and more comprehensive Hutterite Confession in 1545.

[24] This was my journal entry on an Anabaptist Heritage Tour, June 5, 2007.

[25] "Reply to Gellius Faber" in *The Complete Writings of Menno Simons*, 670.

[26] Roth, *Stories*, 152-160.

[27] Becker, *Anabaptist Essentials*.

[28] Siaka Traore in Checole, et.al. *Anabaptist Songs in African Hearts*, 266-267.

[29] The date of Palm Sunday, Easter, and other holy dates are determined by the Julian calendar which was used exclusively until 1582.

[30] I'm sure there are events left out and some dates might be disputable and I'm okay with that; it was a messy, grassroots movement, as already indicated. I have restricted this timeline to events directly involving those who were literally "Anabaptists." I have included more events for the years 1525 to 1527 as they were the "original" years. Check the bibliography for my sources and for further reading.

[31] It is impossible to list all the authors who have influenced the development of my Anabaptist thought over the decades. I have listed here only those sources directly used in this book and those that might be of popular reading interest about Anabaptist origins.

ACKNOWLEDGEMENTS

Just as it seemed appropriate to paint sites related to Anabaptist origins in a simple watercolor folk-art style, it also seems appropriate for a small, Mennonite, family-owned business to be the publisher of this book. Thanks to the folks at Masthof for taking on this unique project, especially Liz Petersheim for her patience, flexibility, and creativity in formatting and design.

Authors always thank their supportive families, but in my case, it was more than just moral support. My four young adult children (Micah, Sarina, Adriel, Joel) all brought their unique artistic and professional skills to this project and helped with editing, scanning, photography, videography, design, and expert opinion. The moral support was provided by my life-partner, Cynthia, who deals with five year olds in the classroom every day, and then has to put up with me "geeking out" over 500-year-old stories when she comes home exhausted! Thanks for loving me the way I am.

A few other people have had direct and tangible contributions to this project. Former students, now friends, Amy Van Bergen, Brett Mathews, and Justin Sun all read an early manuscript and offered critique, affirmation, and advice. Thanks to John Sharp for his personal, wise, and inspiring leadership of Anabaptist Heritage Tours in Europe that I was privileged to be on, and for writing the foreword for this book in the same manner. Thanks to Richard Thiessen, director of the Mennonite Heritage Museum in Abbotsford, BC, who first hosted my exhibition of watercolor paintings and storyboards in the museum gallery.

Those who wrote endorsements for the back cover were not random selections. Audrey Voth Petkau is the president of TourMagination, a company that offers Anabaptist pilgrimage experiences, among other tours. (Thanks to Wilmer Martin who founded the organization and co-led a tour with me.) J. Denny Weaver has been my primary scholarly influence in how I view Anabaptist history and theology, and Stuart Murray's fresh articulation of Anabaptist convictions continues to inspire me. Justin Sun is a young Anabaptist voice you will hear more from in the coming years.

There is always a deeper intangible background to every project. I am thankful for the late Ben Hoeppner for first igniting my interest in Anabaptist origins when I was a 19-year-old college student, and for the late Ian Rennie, who encouraged me to focus my studies in seminary on the history and theology of my own Mennonite tradition, rather than on the broader evangelical world of the seminary. Thanks to Ron Penner, for first inviting me to teach Anabaptist History and Theology at Columbia Bible College. I am thankful for the late Peter Kehler, who raised funds on my behalf, and for members of Emmanuel Mennonite Church who donated, so that I could go on my first Anabaptist Heritage Tour in Europe. I am grateful to be part of this local Anabaptist/Mennonite community of faith.

ABOUT THE AUTHOR

GARETH BRANDT is a freelance artist, itinerant speaker, and independent scholar. He was born in Steinbach, Manitoba, Canada, and has served Mennonite churches in Ontario, Manitoba, Saskatchewan, Alberta, and British Columbia as a congregational and denominational youth pastor and most recently as a college professor teaching spiritual formation and Anabaptist history and theology for more than two decades. Gareth has always enjoyed being creative and has dabbled in various artistic endeavors from poetry to painting and from sculpture to spoken word. Gareth lives with his wife Cynthia, and they are part of Emmanuel Mennonite Church in Abbotsford, BC. They enjoy four adult children, three daughter-in-laws, and one grandchild. You can follow his blog at www.garethbrandt.wordpress.com and listen to some of his poetry at https://www.youtube.com/@GarethBrandt.

www.ingramcontent.com/pod-product-compliance
Lightning Source LLC
Chambersburg PA
CBHW040009080526
44586CB00028B/2945